MY COMMUNITY

A TRIP TO THE FARMERS' MARKET

Jack Reader

PowerKiDS press.

New York

Published in 2017 by The Rosen Publishing Group, Inc.
29 East 21st Street, New York, NY 10010

First Edition

Editor: Melissa Raé Shofner
Book Design: Mickey Harmon

Photo Credits: Cover Hero Images/Getty Images; p. 5 littleny/Shutterstock.com; p. 6 Arina P Habich/Shutterstock.com; p. 9 AmbientShoot/Shutterstock.com; p. 10 Baloncici/Shutterstock.com; p. 13 Image Source/Getty Images; p. 14 youngryand/Shutterstock.com; p. 17 cpaulfell/Shutterstock.com; p. 18 Peter Hendrie/Getty Images; p. 21 Monkey Business Images/Shutterstock.com; p. 22 Education Images/UIG/Getty Images.

Library of Congress Cataloging-in-Publication Data

Names: Reader, Jack, author.
Title: A trip to the farmers' market / Jack Reader.
Other titles: PowerKids readers. My community.
Description: New York : PowerKids Press, [2017] | Series: My community | Includes index.
Identifiers: LCCN 2016027645| ISBN 9781499427790 (pbk. book) | ISBN 9781508152941 (6 pack) | ISBN 9781499430066 (library bound book)
Subjects: LCSH: Farmers' markets–Juvenile literature.
Classification: LCC HD9005 .R43 2017 | DDC 381/.41–dc23
LC record available at https://lccn.loc.gov/2016027645

Manufactured in the United States of America

CPSIA Compliance Information: Batch #BW17PK: For Further Information contact Rosen Publishing, New York, New York at 1-800-237-9932

CONTENTS

The farmers' market is outside.

DAHLIA
LOBELIA

FRESH
LOCAL
PRODUCE

The food is grown nearby.

They sell fruits.

They sell vegetables.

We fill a big bag.

A man plays **guitar**.

We buy **flowers**.

Cybele Honey 500g
Grapefruit Marmalade
Honey 500g
Grapefruit Marmalade
Grapefruit Marmalade
Grapefruit Marmalade
Honey
Honey 500g
Whole Fruit Damson Jam
Marmalade 500g
Grapefruit Marmalade
Honey

There is honey and jam.

A woman sells fresh **bread**.

Our own
Fresh picked
onions
$1.00/lb.
Our own
Fresh picked
eggplant
$2.00/lb.
Our Own
Fresh Picked
Red Potatoes
$1.50/LB

There is so much to see!

WORDS TO KNOW

bread

flowers

guitar

INDEX

WEBSITES

Due to the changing nature of Internet links, PowerKids Press has developed an online list of websites related to the subject of this book. This site is updated regularly. Please use this link to access the list: www.powerkidslinks.com/mycom/market